T0207945

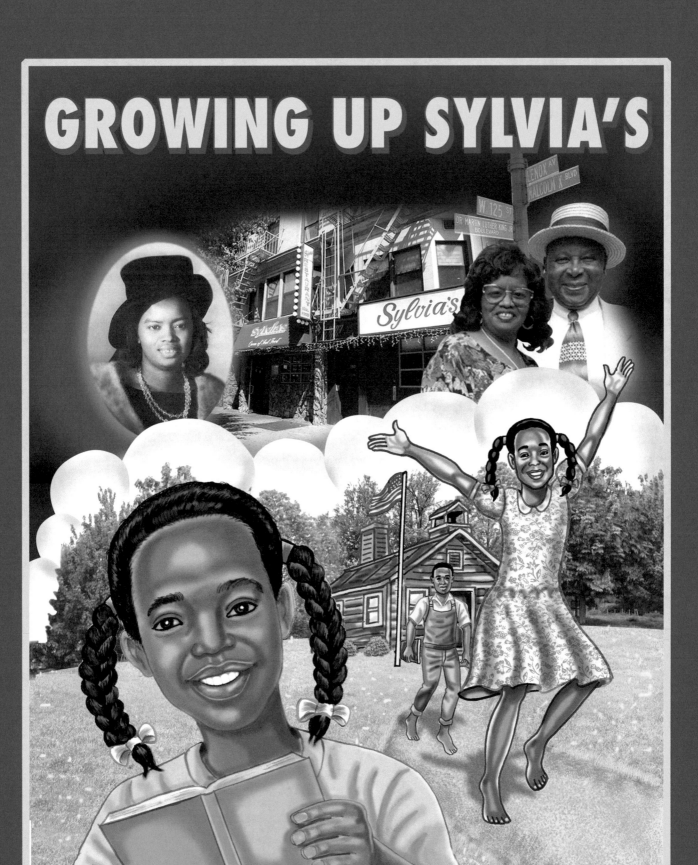

GROWING UP SYLVIA'S

By Brenda Woods and Van D. Woods
Illustrations By Laurel Tyndale

AuthorHouse™
1663 Liberty Drive
Bloomington, IN 47403
www.authorhouse.com
Phone: 1 (800) 839-8640

Published by AuthorHouse 02/27/2018

ISBN: 978-1-5462-3055-7 (sc)
ISBN: 978-1-5462-3056-4 (e)

Library of Congress Control Number: 2018902290

Print information available on the last page.

This book is printed on acid-free paper.

authorHOUSE®

Sylvia Woods/The Queen of Soul Food
"If these feet could talk!"
Sylvia Woods

Published by Brenda Woods and Van D. Woods
Lake City, South Carolina 29560
Text copyright © 1999, by Brenda Woods and Van D. Woods
All rights reserved. Historical text

Growing Up Sylvia's

Brenda and Van D. Woods

This story is based on the lives of the family of Sylvia and Herbert Woods from Sylvia's Restaurant in Harlem, New York. This book is for young readers and adult readers and includes reading activities for students and teachers.

In this book, readers will explore and relate to a journey of success and happiness of an American family. Sylvia and Herbert came from a humble background in the South, in Hemingway, South Carolina, and became the owners of a multimillion-dollar enterprise in the North.

We hope you enjoy reading about this wonderful American family who represents what can be done with faith, love, determination, and unity within a family.

One blustery sunny day in Hemingway, South Carolina, in the late 1930s, twelve-year-old Sylvia Pressley played barefoot in a large bean field on her mother's farm. Sylvia and her mother, Ms. Julia Pressley, and her adopted sister, Louise, lived alone on the farm. Sylvia's father, Mr. Van Pressley, was a World War I veteran who had died from a war-related illness when she was a baby. Her mother and other family members helped in taking care of the farmland and the livestock.

Sylvia was born in Hemingway on February 2, 1926. She was a beautiful young girl who loved her family and wished to have a family of her own when she was older. Sylvia had brown eyes and skin like a mahogany tree. Her hair was as black as the ebony keys on a piano. She loved to run in the bean field barefoot. The soil beneath her feet felt soft. The soil was a warm, fluffy rug that made Sylvia smile when she felt the softness beneath her feet. Sylvia had a smile that could brighten up any room when she was present. Sylvia liked to play, and she liked to help her mother on their farm.

Every morning, Sylvia would get up early to prepare breakfast for her mother. Sometimes, her sister, Louise, would help. Louise was a relative who was adopted by Ms. Julia. Louise and Sylvia were very close. Ms. Julia was a midwife. She assisted mothers with delivering their babies. During the early 1900s in the South, many babies were delivered at home, not with doctors, but with midwives. It was more affordable for African Americans to deliver their babies at home than to go to a hospital. Besides, during this time, there were not many African American doctors in the South. Many white doctors in the South did not have African American patients. Ms. Julia delivered many babies, and she also made sure the birth certificates were filed and copies were given to the mothers. Ms. Julia became well known for her occupation, and many of her clients called her "Mamma."

After breakfast each morning, Sylvia would clean up and head for school. Sylvia and Louise would walk down a sandy dirt road to get there. Sometimes, they would meet up with their best friend, Willa. Sylvia was very pleased to have a sister and to have a great friend like Willa. The three of them were like three peas in a pod. They often walked to school together.

The school was a one-room building built out of unpainted wooden boards. It had six windows, with three windows on each side of the building and two doors. The school had one door for entering and one for exiting. There was an outhouse, a building outside the main building used as a restroom. These restrooms were much different from the restrooms we have today. There was no electric switch or septic tank in the outhouse or in the school. For light, they used an oil lamp and lanterns.

A stove that used wood and matches was used to cook the food and to keep warm. This was the only heating system they had. There were five teachers for grades one through eight. During the early 1900s, every state required students to complete elementary school. Sylvia loved going to school, and she loved learning new things.

During recess time, Sylvia would play hide-and-seek with her two best friends, and they would play house, pretending to be a mother and children. Sylvia always wanted to be the mother. They would pretend that the father was away on business, and Louise and Willa would play the children. After playing house, Sylvia would get a long stick that had fallen from a tree in the schoolyard and draw in the sand. She would draw a picture of a family with a father, mother, and children. Her friends would also draw pictures in the sand of animals, dolls, and doll dresses. They enjoyed expressing their dreams by drawing pictures in the sand.

Autumn came, and one breezy day as the wind blew silently, Sylvia was outside during recess time, drawing in the sand. A kid asked her, "Why do you always draw pictures of a family?" At that moment, Sylvia looked up and saw a very slim, brown-skinned boy standing over her.

She cleared her throat and answered, "I like to draw pictures of families in the sand. You see, my father died when I was very young, and I miss having a father around. I want to have a family of my own when I grow up. I also have a big dream of owning a beauty salon business someday. By the way, what is your name?"

"My name is Herbert, Herbert Woods."

"Nice to meet you, Herbert Woods," Sylvia replied.

"And your name?"

"Well, my name is Sylvia Pressley."

"It is indeed a pleasure to meet you, Miss Sylvia Pressley," Herbert said.

They both laughed.

"I will be over on this side of the yard tomorrow during recess time, and I hope to see you here, Miss Sylvia," said Herbert.

"You just keep hoping, Mr. Herbert," Sylvia said with a smile on her face.

When Herbert arrived home later that day, he was anxious to tell his parents about the young lady he had met at school. Herbert was also trying to figure out in his head where he had seen Sylvia before. He knew in his heart that he had seen her before, but the memory of his first vision of Sylvia was not registering with him. His parents knew

Ms. Julia, Sylvia's mother, and they were pleased to know that their son was making friends at school.

Herbert's parents, Mr. Herbert Woods Sr. and Mrs. Pearl Woods, were well educated. Mr. Woods was a minister, and Mrs. Woods was a schoolteacher. They were also farmers. They owned several acres of land in Hemingway, South Carolina, which they lived on and farmed. Herbert had one brother, James, and one sister, Annette. Herbert was the oldest of the three children. Herbert also helped out on the farm, and he loved to read.

For the next several years at school, Sylvia and Herbert would sit on a tree trunk and talk during recess time and share their lunch. They became inseparable. They often spent time together during and after school. Herbert would walk Sylvia home every day. Many times, Willa and Louise were present on their walks home. Willa and Louise embraced Sylvia and Herbert's friendship. They liked having Herbert around.

One day, while Sylvia and Herbert were sitting on Ms. Julia's porch, Herbert finally remembered where he and Sylvia had first met. It was in one of the bean fields on Ms. Julia's farm the previous summer. They were gathering beans for their family and to make extra money. On their first encounter, they did not speak. They just glanced at each other from the bean row that stood between them. Herbert shared their first encounter with Sylvia, and she laughed and said, "You're right. I do remember that day in the bean field. I looked for you after we got through picking beans, and you were nowhere to be found. I'm glad that we found each other again. Now tell me, Herbert, what do you want to do when you finish school?"

"Hmm, I'm not sure about what I want to do, but I have read a lot of information about the navy. I enjoyed learning about how to become a sailor on a ship. You can cook for the navy and fight for them too. Miss Sylvia, I think I want to join the navy," answered Herbert.

"Isn't that kind of dangerous? You could be killed by soldiers from other countries who disagree with our country, or your ship might sink to the bottom of the ocean," Sylvia said anxiously.

"Nonsense, Miss Sylvia, those things ain't happening to me. I am going be a sailor and sail across the big blue sea like the Vikings and Christopher Columbus," said Herbert.

Sylvia just smiled and said, "I am going to cosmetology school. I want to own a beauty salon business someday."

"Wow, Miss Sylvia, that sounds *big!* How would you get there?" Herbert asked.

"I'm not sure. Just like you, I know this is what I want to do, and I'm going to make sure it happens," said Sylvia.

"Just maybe we could go to New York City together after we graduate from school," said Herbert.

"That sounds like a plan," Sylvia responded.

One evening just before dark in the fall of 1941, Sylvia and Ms. Julia were sitting on the porch of their home, watching the scenery of the farmland and listening to the sounds of the night casting over the farm like a gigantic dark cloud. Sylvia turned to Ms. Julia and said, "Momma, I want to go to New York City to attend cosmetology school after I graduate from school."

Ms. Julia responded, "Baby, why so far away?"

"Well, Momma, New York City has the best beauty school for black people. I am old enough to take care of myself now, and you have sacrificed so much for me. Momma, I am ready to make you proud of me," Sylvia said.

"Sugar, I am already proud of you," said Ms. Julia.

"Besides, Momma, I have heard that New York City is where black folks can get a good education to help with starting a business. I enjoy styling hair and applying makeup, and there are so many people in New York who need their hair and makeup done. I would fit right in there, Momma," Sylvia said excitedly.

Ms. Julia looked at Sylvia, and for the first time, she saw Sylvia not as her little girl anymore, but as a beautiful and ambitious young lady who was eager to fulfill her dreams. "I will have to think about this more, honey. Let's go to bed now. We can discuss this later," said Ms. Julia.

Sylvia had a long, weary night. She said her prayers and tried to fall asleep, but she was worried that her mother would not agree to let her move to New York City.

The next day, Ms. Julia did not have an answer for Sylvia. Sylvia did not ask her mother about moving to New York City again, but Sylvia was anxious to know. Sylvia had another sleepless night. She really wanted to move to New York City to attend cosmetology school. "Momma just gotta say yes!" Sylvia whispered to herself.

Morning came, and after they had breakfast, Ms. Julia suggested, "Sylvia, let's go for a walk." Sylvia agreed.

They walked along the bean fields on the farm. They walked by the old barn with the large barbed-wire fence, where the livestock was kept. Sylvia could smell the fragrances of the farm, and she noticed the scenery around the farmhouse.

The farmland was all shades of green, orange, brown, and yellow. It was a beautiful sight, with the blue sky and the bright sun shining above in the cool breeze. Sylvia closed her eyes as the breeze refreshed her face. She felt awake and ready for the world. Sylvia realized that this was home, and no matter where she went or lived, this would always be her home, her safe haven.

Sylvia's reflection of the love she shared with her mom and other family members on the farm made her feel a sense of belonging to a family that was both beautiful and extraordinary.

Ms. Julia took Sylvia's hand and said, "I think you should move to New York to attend cosmetology school."

Sylvia beamed from ear to ear. With tears in her eyes, Sylvia gave her mom a kiss and a big, tight hug and said, "Oh, thank you, Momma! I will make you so proud, and I will write to you every week."

"You better!" Ms. Julia said with a big smile. "Now, before you can go, young lady, I must write my relatives, Walter and Mary in Brooklyn, New York, to ask them to let you stay with them while you attend school," Ms. Julia said.

"Oh, thank you, thank you, Momma," Sylvia said happily.

Later, Sylvia's excitement became mixed emotions. She was excited and happy about moving to New York City, but she realized she would be leaving her mom, family members, the farm, her friends, and most of all, she would be leaving Herbert. In the meantime, Ms. Julia wrote a letter to her relatives, Walter and Mary, in New York. Now Sylvia would have to wait for a response from them.

Spring came, and Sylvia and Herbert were graduating in a month. They were both excited about graduating and starting their careers. One day outside of the school, Sylvia finally told Herbert the news about her mom agreeing to let her move to New York City. Herbert had some news of his own to tell Sylvia. "That's wonderful, Sylvia! I, too, hope to be stationed in New York when I enlist in the navy. Maybe we both will be in New York City at the same time."

Sylvia looked at Herbert and gave him a big smile and replied, "That would be wonderful, Herbert. Just think, both of us in New York City!"

They laughed. Then Herbert continued, "With the both of us together, the sky is the limit. We can do this, Sylvia!" They then embraced and went inside the school to join the others.

In the spring of 1941, after Sylvia and Herbert had graduated from school, Ms. Julia received a letter from her relatives in Brooklyn, New York. The letter informed Ms. Julia and Sylvia that they would love to have Sylvia stay with them while she attended cosmetology school. The only problem was that Sylvia would have to leave the next day to get enrolled into the school. Sylvia was excited and sad. She realized that the move was happening quicker than she expected. She would not have time to say her good-byes to her friends and family. Later that evening, Sylvia began to pack for New York.

The next morning, after breakfast, Ms. Julia drove Sylvia, dressed in her Sunday best, down a long dirt road to the train station in a Mercury car. Ms. Julia had kept her husband's car and taught herself how to drive. Sylvia watched the dust as it gathered behind the car along the dirt road. She was missing home already. When they arrived at the train station, passengers were boarding the train. Sylvia said good-bye to Ms. Julia. Ms. Julia hugged Sylvia and gave her a brown paper bag with her lunch inside and said, "Oh, my baby, I will miss you, and I love you very much. Mind your manners, and listen to Walter and Mary. They will be your parents until you return. Take care of yourself, baby!"

"Yes, Momma, I will, and I love you. Thanks for everything. I will write to you soon!" Sylvia said affectionately.

"Go on now, baby!" Ms. Julia said with tears in her eyes.

Sylvia boarded the train from the rear. Blacks in the South in were not allowed to sit in the front of the train with white passengers. Blacks were under a law called *separate but equal*. They did not have the same rights or privileges as whites. Blacks were given more rights after the Civil Rights Act of 1964 was passed. As the train departed from the station, Sylvia waved good-bye to Ms. Julia until she was out of sight. Ms. Julia cried the entire journey back home.

After twenty-four hours on the train, Sylvia arrived in New York City. Walter and Mary and their two children met Sylvia outside the station. They greeted her with a big, warm hug. The climate of New York welcomed Sylvia also. Sylvia had to pull out her coat from her suitcase because the spring temperature felt cool to her.

The crowded city, with its different kinds of vehicles, large buildings, and so many people, caught Sylvia's attention. To Sylvia, watching the people of New York City was like watching an anthill in the South when it is tampered with. The ants racing around the anthill was how Sylvia saw the people of New York City. Sylvia, Walter, Mary, and their two children walked the three blocks to where Walter had parked the car to go to their home in Brooklyn. Sylvia was captivated by the large skyscrapers and how all the buildings were connected in each block they walked. New York City was more than Sylvia could ever have imagined. Back home, neighbors lived miles away from each other, and neighbors in New York City live in the same building or next door. Stores and businesses were within walking distance, and some were just down the block from Walter and Mary's home.

The climate of New York was very different from Hemingway, South Carolina. The New York City climate was much colder in the fall, winter, and spring. Sylvia had to get used to the new climate. In the city, there were so many things to see and do. Sylvia smiled so much that her jaws and lips were tingling. She was mesmerized with the shops, museums, and theaters she visited in the city. Sylvia was trying to adjust to living in a big city in the North, which was very different from living on a farm in the South. She would be starting beauty school in a week. After two days in her new home, Sylvia sat down one evening and wrote her mother a letter.

Mary had sent Ms. Julia a telegram on the day Sylvia arrived, to inform her that Sylvia had made it to New York City safely. Ms. Julia was very pleased. In Sylvia's letter to Ms. Julia, she expressed how much she missed her, and she told her mother about the different sights she had seen in New York City. She closed her letter with "Love you, Momma! P.S.: Please tell Herbert where I am!"

Back in South Carolina, Herbert visited Ms. Julia, who was surprised to see him. "Hello, Ms. Julia. Have you heard from Sylvia? How is she?" Herbert said anxiously.

"Come on in, Herbert, I will fix you a sandwich, and we can talk about Sylvia," said Ms. Julia.

Herbert and Ms. Julia sat at the kitchen table, and while Herbert ate his sandwich, she told him that Sylvia was now living in New York with relatives and she would attend cosmetology school while she was there. Herbert began to think of ways to get to New York. He thanked Ms. Julia for the sandwich and for the information about Sylvia. He got up from the kitchen table, said good-bye to Ms. Julia, and left quickly.

On his way home, Herbert decided to enlist in the navy earlier than he had planned to, hoping he would be stationed in New York. He was not old enough to enlist, so he lied about his age on the enlistment form, saying that he was eighteen years old, when he was really only sixteen. He wanted the opportunity to get to New York to see Sylvia.

Herbert's parents were upset and worried about their son enlisting in the navy. They tried to get him to retract the enlistment, but it was too late. He was shipped out before they could stop him. Unfortunately, Herbert was stationed in Norfolk, Virginia, and later, he was shipped to California. He was a cook on the ship. Herbert was very disappointed, but he was still determined to get to New York to see Sylvia.

In New York, Sylvia attended school during the day. She was also missing her mom and Herbert. Sylvia studied for many hours during the day. She was determined to reach her goal of becoming the owner of a beauty salon.

One year later, as Sylvia was walking home, she saw a young man in a navy uniform, sitting on the stoop of her relatives' home. She stopped in her tracks. She took a closer look and realized it was Herbert. She quickly ran to him and gave him a huge hug, almost knocking him over. *He looks so handsome!* Sylvia thought.

Sylvia and Herbert took a walk down the block from her relatives' home, and they embraced. They were happy to see each other. Sylvia recognized Herbert's uniform and said, "You joined the navy, I see."

"Yes, I did. I wanted to see you, so I enlisted early in hope that I would be stationed in New York City, but I was sent to Norfolk, Virginia, for a year. It took me this long to get here. We are here on a special mission. We will ship out in five days," Herbert said.

"I am very happy to see you," said Sylvia.

They held hands, and as they walked, they could hear music from a small blues band performing on the sidewalk. The streets were crowded with people, cars, and buses. The brownstone buildings on both sides of the street looked like boxes of chocolate to Herbert. "It is beautiful but noisy here," Herbert said.

"Yes, it is," responded Sylvia.

They saw an entrance and an exit tunnel to an underground subway station, and they could see numerous people going in and out. "Have you ever taken the subway?" Herbert asked.

"Yes, I have. I take it home every day from school," Sylvia said.

"I have never taken a subway," said Herbert.

"Oh, you will, Herbert. I promise," said Sylvia.

Herbert and Sylvia walked and talked for hours. It was time for Herbert to get back to his crew's ship. They made plans to see each other the next day.

The next day, Herbert returned and told Sylvia that he was shipping out the next morning. Sylvia was disappointed. She hoped they would have more time to spend together. Herbert also hoped for more time with Sylvia. They took a walk down to the subway station. Herbert took his first ride on an underground subway train. They got off and walked three blocks to the park.

While walking in the park, Herbert said, "Sylvia, I have something to ask you."

"What is it, Herbert?" Sylvia said with a motionless face.

Then Herbert reached inside his pants pocket and pulled out a small box. Sylvia's eyes widened, and her was heart beating like a drum. The look on her face became a smile.

Herbert got down on one knee, handed Sylvia the small box, and said, "Will you marry me?"

Even though Sylvia's heart was beating fast, she was able to mutter, "Yes! Yes, I will marry you, Herbert!" Sylvia opened the small box, and there in the sunlight was the most beautiful ring she had ever seen. "It's beautiful!" she said happily.

Herbert stood up and placed the ring on Sylvia's finger. They embraced and kissed.

"I will wear this ring forever," said Sylvia.

Unfortunately, Herbert had to leave again. Sylvia was sad to watch him go. Later that night, Sylvia held the hand with the ring all night long, and in her dreams, she could visualize Herbert proposing to her in the park. It was comforting to Sylvia to remember Herbert's marriage proposal.

Two days later, Herbert appeared again at Sylvia's relatives' home. He had asked his captain for more leave time, and his captain agreed. Sylvia was thrilled to see Herbert, and Herbert was content with his decision to spend more time with Sylvia. They spend all of his leave time together. Then it was time for Herbert to return to the sea and for

Sylvia to finish cosmetology school. Sylvia graduated in 1943 and returned home to Hemingway, South Carolina. One year later, Herbert returned home to Hemingway, and he and Sylvia were married in 1944.

One year after they were married, they had their first child, a son they named Van. Herbert returned to the sea during World War II, and Sylvia started a beautician business in Hemingway. Sylvia's business was located on her farmland. A wash and press with a style cost one dollar and fifty cents, and just a wash was 75 cents. Sylvia was one of the first African American beauticians in Hemingway. Many customers from Hemingway and the surrounding areas came to Sylvia's Salon to get their hair done and to visit with Sylvia while she worked. Sylvia made a great sum of money. A dollar could buy so much more during the 1940s than it does today. Sylvia was determined to make a good life for her new family. Herbert and Sylvia kept in touch through letters.

In 1946, Herbert had survived the war and received a medical discharge from the navy. He and Sylvia decided to move back to New York City because jobs were more available for African American men in New York. So, they moved to Harlem, and Herbert took a job as a taxi driver. Sylvia continued with her hair salon business. She worked on people's hair in their apartment building in Harlem. This was convenient for Sylvia because two years later, she and Herbert had their second child, a daughter, Bedelia. Sylvia worked at home and took care of their young children. She had always wanted a family of her own, and now she finally had one. Sylvia was pleased with her new life.

In the early 1950s, the family was exposed to some hardships. They needed more money to live in the city. Herbert's taxi-driving job had ended, and Sylvia decided to take a job at an appliance factory in Manhattan, New York, to help with the expenses. Herbert found another job as a city cab driver. Herbert worked late hours, and the children stayed with relatives until Sylvia got home. Sometimes Sylvia was exhausted from working in the factory, but she would never complain about her job. She was just thankful that they could make ends meet and her children were well taken care of. They later had a third child, another son, Kenneth. Sylvia's family was growing, and she was concerned about how she and Herbert would provide for and protect their family.

One evening in 1958, while Sylvia was walking home from work, she was tired, so she decided to go into the café on Lenox Avenue to rest for a spell. While sitting there, Sylvia mustered up enough courage to inquire about a job working in the café.

"Hello, miss. What can I get for you?" a man at the café counter asked.

"I'm here seeking employment," said Sylvia.

"Yes, miss, are you interested in applying for a job?" the man at counter asked.

"Yes, sir," replied Sylvia.

"Do you have any experience?" the man asked.

"No," said Sylvia.

The man looked at Sylvia and noticed that she was very petite but confident. Then he said, "What is your name, miss?"

"Sylvia Woods. Yes, that's my name," Sylvia said boldly.

"It's nice to meet you, Ms. Sylvia Woods. My name is Mr. Johnson." At that moment, a lovely lady came over to the counter and stood next to Mr. Johnson. "This is my wife, Vicky, and we are the owners of this establishment."

"Nice to meet you, Mr. Johnson and Mrs. Johnson, and by the way, my name is Mrs. Sylvia Woods!"

"Oh, I do apologize for that error," responded Mr. Johnson.

"Apology accepted," Sylvia said.

"When can you start?" Mr. Johnson asked.

"I can start right away," answered Sylvia.

"All right then, I will see you tomorrow morning at eight o'clock," said Mr. Johnson.

"I will be here tomorrow on time," said Sylvia.

Sylvia told Herbert about her new job. Herbert was supportive of Sylvia starting a new job that was more comfortable and enjoyable for her. Sylvia and Herbert loved to cook. Sylvia knew that now she would have the opportunity to prepare some of her southern meals at Johnson's Café. The thought of cooking and serving others made Sylvia feel like she had found what she really wanted to do in life.

The next morning, Sylvia got up early, made breakfast for her family and waited for her cousin to come over to babysit the children. Then she headed off to her new job. She did not notify her old employer about her new job. She wanted to wait and see if the new job worked out. She just didn't show up at her old job. Sylvia walked to the corner of 131st Street and then walked four blocks to her new job. Sylvia was excited about having a new job at the café.

The Johnsons' café was known for serving burgers, fries, rice, chicken, vegetables, pork chops, and many other southern dishes. Sylvia's first job was to make and serve the coffee. Sylvia made great coffee for the customers, and she enjoyed meeting the many different customers who came to the café. She greeted each customer with a smile and a warm hello. The customers really liked the new waitress.

After two weeks of her working at the café, the customers would request Sylvia to wait on them, and they would leave generous tips for her. Sylvia's tips were a blessing to her and her family. She felt good about what she was doing at the café, and her boss, Mr. Johnson, noticed that the café was a lot busier since Sylvia began working there.

Before long, Sylvia was running the restaurant. She became head waitress, and soon after that, Mr. Johnson allowed Sylvia to cook. She introduced many of her southern recipes. She made fried chicken, baked chicken, and smothered chicken with potatoes and gravy. She also made grits, as well as salmon croquettes with steamed vegetables and beans. Two of her favorite dishes were her sweet cornbread and barbequed ribs. The customers loved the sweet cornbread. They loved it with their meals or with a cup of coffee. They enjoyed Sylvia's southern cuisine. The customers would ask to meet the cook after eating one of Sylvia's dishes. She enjoyed cooking, meeting the customers, and satisfying their appetites.

In 1961, on a busy day at the café, Mr. Johnson called Sylvia into his office. "Have a seat, Sylvia. Take a load off," Mr. Johnson said.

Sylvia was concerned about what her boss wanted to talk to her about. Sylvia took a seat in front of Mr. Johnson's desk.

He smiled and said, "Sylvia, my wife and I have noticed how hard you have been working and how well you are running our restaurant business. We think you would make a great manager and owner of this establishment."

"What do you mean, Mr. Johnson?" Sylvia asked.

"Well, we want to sell our business. My wife and I are moving to upstate New York to build a resort business for black people. We wanted to offer the business to you for a reasonable price," responded Mr. Johnson.

Sylvia was stunned and speechless. She did not say a word for about two minutes.

"Well, what do you think? Sylvia, are you interested in buying the café?" Mr. Johnson asked.

Sylvia finally spoke. "I will have to talk to my husband about it, and we will let you know our decision."

Mr. Johnson agreed to give Sylvia time to think about it and to discuss it with her husband, Herbert.

Sylvia could not believe what just happened. She was asked to be the owner of a restaurant. This was beyond any dreams she had ever had. She always saw herself being successful in a beauty shop business, but not in her wildest dreams did she ever see herself owning a restaurant. Sylvia finished up her rounds in the restaurant and headed home to tell Herbert the news. As she walked to the front door of Johnson's Cafe, she spotted Herbert sitting outside in his city cab. He waited for Sylvia to get off work because he was in the area on a break.

The city cab job was a struggle for Herbert, but he was determined to make money to help take care of his family. Sylvia ran to the cab, got in, and gave Herbert a kiss. Then she asked him, "How was your day?"

 "It is a great day, now that I get to take my lovely wife home," Herbert responded.

Sylvia smiled and said, "You really know how to make your wife feel like she is the luckiest woman in the world." Sylvia did not talk about the restaurant offer her bosses made to her until they were home.

Later that same night, after supper, Sylvia said excitedly, "Honey, you won't believe what my boss asked me today."

"What did he ask you, Sylvia?"

"Well, he asked me if we wanted to buy the restaurant," Sylvia replied.

"Are you serious?" Herbert asked.

"Yeah! He wants to sell the restaurant because he and his wife are moving to upstate New York to start a resort real-estate business for blacks. Ain't that something?" Sylvia said.

"Sylvia, do you know what this means for our family? To have our own business is to be powerful and successful. I like the idea of owning a restaurant because we both love to cook, and we are good cooks. We could do this together, Sylvia," said Herbert.

"There is just one problem. Where are we going to get the money to buy the restaurant?" Sylvia asked.

"How much money do we have saved so far?" Herbert asked.

"We have two thousand dollars saved. That's not enough to buy the restaurant," Sylvia said.

Herbert embraced Sylvia and said, "We will get through this, and we will be successful with our restaurant."

Sylvia smiled in agreement.

The next day, Mr. Johnson asked Sylvia what she and her husband decided to do about the restaurant offer. Sylvia informed him that they were considering buying the restaurant, but they were having a problem getting the money to purchase the restaurant. Mr. Johnson asked Sylvia, "Do you and your husband have any collateral?"

"What's that, sir?" Sylvia asked.

"Collateral is like money or property used as security for a loan from a bank," said Mr. Johnson.

"We don't, sir, but my mother does. She has property in South Carolina. It is a small farm," answered Sylvia.

"Why don't you ask your mother to use your farmland as collateral for a loan to buy the restaurant?" Mr. Johnson asked.

Sylvia talked with Herbert about asking Ms. Julia to use her farm as collateral for a loan. Herbert agreed on one condition: that they would pay the loan off as soon as possible, and Ms. Julia would not be responsible for making any payments for this loan.

Ms. Julia's home was now wired with electricity, and she had a telephone in her home. She was delighted to hear Sylvia and Herbert's voices over the phone. Sylvia told her mom the news about the restaurant. Ms. Julia agreed to take out a mortgage on the farm to help with the payment of the restaurant. Ms. Julia was proud of Sylvia and Herbert's achievements. She was always there to give them love and support. Sylvia loved her mom, and Herbert loved her almost as much as Sylvia did. After receiving the funds for the restaurant, Sylvia and Herbert took the money they saved along with the loan Ms. Julia got from the bank and purchased Johnson's Café on 126th and Lenox Avenue in Harlem, New York in 1962 during the era of the Civil Rights Movement.

They changed the name of the restaurant to Sylvia's Restaurant. The menu at Sylvia's Restaurant consisted of southern cooking. Sylvia's grew from a one-room restaurant with a counter to a three-room restaurant and a catering hall. Sylvia and Herbert worked side by side in their new restaurant. Sylvia's Restaurant grew and grew. People from all over the United States and other countries, including celebrities, politicians, and presidents all dined at Sylvia's Restaurant.

In 1968, Sylvia and Herbert had their fourth child, another daughter they named Crizette. Sylvia's continued to grow and grow after they purchased the restaurant property. Many years later, two of the older children, Bedelia and Kenneth, helped out in the restaurant. Sylvia's family and their restaurant business blossomed. Their oldest son, Van, started a line of Sylvia's canned food products and spices in 1994, which were being sold in major supermarkets all over the country.

Sylvia and Herbert also started a real-estate business, and with Van's help, they now owned the entire block of real estate from 126th to 127th on Lenox Avenue in Harlem in New York City. Sylvia has two major cookbooks with recipes you can prepare at home.

Sylvia grew up to become known as the Queen of Soul Food of Harlem. Sylvia Pressley Woods got more than she could ever imagine. She got the beautiful family she always wanted and a successful business that she loved. Sylvia's became an icon to the world, and Sylvia Woods became a major entrepreneur in New York City.

Sylvia and Herbert Woods came from humble beginnings and became entrepreneurs of a multimillion-dollar business in Harlem, New York. Herbert Woods died in 2001. Sylvia missed her husband deeply, and she and her four children, grandchildren, and great-grandchildren continued to serve the customers delicious southern cooking with southern hospitality, which expanded the Sylvia Woods legacy.

If you ask Sylvia how she did it, she would say it was with hard work, love of family, friends, customers, and most of all, her faith. *Growing Up Sylvia's* is the foundation of a multimillion-dollar enterprise of an African American family from Hemingway, South Carolina, to Harlem, New York. Sylvia Woods, the Queen of Soul Food, died on July 19, 2012 at the age of eighty-six.

The Woods Family

In memory
of
Sylvia, Herbert, and Ms. Julia

Ms. Julia died in 1987.
Herbert Woods died in 2001.
Sylvia Woods died on July 19, 2012.

Sylvia Woods in 1960

Herbert and Sylvia in New York

The Curriculum for *Growing Up Sylvia's*
Reading Comprehension Components

Skills
Main Idea/Supportive Details

Cause/Effect
Context Clues
Draw Conclusion
Compare/Contrast
Figurative Language

Writing Skills Component
*Book Report (Five questions: Who? What? When? Where? Why? How? A Summary Statement)
*Story Map
*Informational Web for Research of the Civil Rights Era, Sights of New York City, or life in the
South and the North

*Essay (paragraph writing on a topic related to the story and life experiences.) Sylvia wanted to become a beautician, and she did because she was ambitious and determined. She also became the Queen of Soul Food and the owner of a multimillion-dollar business that included a restaurant, real-estate businesses, and a line of canned/packaged food products.
Prompts: What do want to do when you grow up? Tell what it is. Why you want to do this? How will you reach this goal? Who or what will help you to reach this goal? Write a conclusion explaining how you will use your achievements.

Vocabulary Words to focus on:
Family
Midwife
Entrepreneur
Outhouse
Recipes
Collateral
Mahogany
Beautician
Cuisine
Ambitious
Rear
Determined

(Activity worksheets on the next pages)
There are many other skills that can be used with this text. Teachers and students may use the text to assist with the reading comprehension and writing standards.

Reading Comprehension Activities for *Growing Up Sylvia's*

Read each question and choose the best answer for each. You may look back in the text to help you complete activities.

(Main Idea/Details)

1. Which detail supports this idea? Ms. Julia was a midwife.
   (A) Ms. Julia was a middle wife.
   (B) Ms. Julia delivered babies in homes.
   (C) Ms. Julia worked at a hospital in the neighborhood.
   (D) Ms. Julia was a medical doctor.

2. Sylvia loves to play barefooted. Which detail supports this idea?
   (A) Sylvia is a beautiful young girl.
   (B) Sylvia has a big smile.
   (C) Sylvia has brown eyes and skin like a mahogany tree.
   (D She smiles when she feels the soft soil beneath her feet.

(Cause/Effect)

3. Sylvia got up early every morning to:
   (A) Fix her hair and her sister's hair.
   (B) Feed the farm animals.
   (C) Prepare breakfast for her family.
   (D) Take a walk around the farm before going to school.

4. Why did all students have to complete elementary school?
   (A) It was required by every state.
   (B) It was required by some states.
   (C) Students love to go to school.
   (D) Students did not have to complete all subjects.

Word Meaning (Context Clues)

5. In the text, Sylvia was ambitious. Which statement is an example of the word *ambitious*?
   (A) To give up.
   (B) To be eager to succeed.
   (C) To make worse.
   (D) To be happy for others.

6. In the text, Mr. Johnson told Sylvia that she needed collateral to buy the restaurant. What is the meaning of the word *collateral* in this sentence?
   (A) Food for the customers.
   (B) More recipes.
   (C) Property.
   (D) Another job.

7. Sylvia and Herbert became entrepreneurs. *Entrepreneurs* in this sentence means:
   (A) Ministers of a church.
   (B) Owners of a business.
   (C) Sailors on a ship.
   (D) Friends.

8. The text said Sylvia and Herbert were inseparable. What does this mean?

(A) They were different people.   (C) They were separate.

(B) They could not be separated.   (D) They were the same.

(Draw Conclusion)

9. Herbert enlisted in the navy at a younger age. What can we conclude about this?
   (A) He was eager to join the navy.   (C) He wanted a trip to the Big Apple.
   (B) Sylvia told him to join the navy.   (D) He was determined to get to see Sylvia in New York.

10. Sylvia only has an adopted sister. What can we conclude?
    (A) Sylvia doesn't have any brothers.   (C) Sylvia loved her sister.
    (B) Sylvia wanted a brother.   (D) Sylvia wanted a family.

11. Sylvia came from humble beginnings and became the Queen of Soul Food. What can we conclude about Sylvia?
    (A) She was poor.   (C) She was not successful.
    (B) She was determined.   (D) She was successful.

12. Why do you think Sylvia continued to work when she had young children at home?
_____

_____

(Compare/Contrast)

13. Use the Venn diagram to compare and contrast the two settings, Hemingway and Harlem, New York.
Write your answers in the circles.

Same

@@@Diagram

Figurative Language

Read and identify the figurative language. Underline the figurative language in the passages from the story. Then choose the correct figurative language for each passage.

Sylvia is a beautiful young girl who loves her family and hopes to have a family of her own when she is older. Sylvia has brown eyes and skin like a mahogany tree. She likes to play and help her mother on their farm.

14. Which example of figurative language is found in this passage?
   (A) Metaphor   (B) Simile   (C) Personification   (D) Hyperbole

Sylvia loves to run in the bean field barefooted. The soil beneath her feet feels soft. The soil is like a warm, fluffy rug underneath her feet, which makes Sylvia smile when she feels the soft soil between her toes.

15. Which example of figurative language is found in this passage?
  (A) Personification   (B) Idiom   (C) Simile   (D) Metaphor

Sylvia was pleased to have a sister, Louise, and a best friend, Willa. They were three peas in a tripod, instead of two peas in a pod.

16. Which example of figurative language is found in this passage?
  (A) Idiom   (B) Personification   (C) Metaphor   (D) Hyperbole

Write three other examples of figurative language from the story.

Glossary

family (n) A unit consisting of parents and children.

midwife (n) A person who assists women in childbirth.

entrepreneur (n) A person who organizes and operates a business.

outhouse (n) An outdoor restroom or toilet.

recipes (n) Directions and ingredients for preparing and cooking food.

appetite (n) A desire for food.

beautician (n) A person who cuts and styles hair.

cuisines (n) Styles and types of food.

mahogany (n/adj) A reddish-brown smooth wood.

mesmerized (v/adj) To be hypnotized or to capture one's attention.

inseparable (adj) Unable to separate or break apart.

Meet the Authors

Brenda Woods is an Administrator in at Elementary School in Lake City, SC with master's degree in Education. Brenda is the wife of Sylvia Woods's oldest son, Van. Brenda and Van have two children, Sierra Sylvia and Devaughn Dax. She enjoys helping students to learn and to succeed as lifelong learners.

Van D. Woods is one of the owners of Sylvia's Enterprises, with a master's degree in business. Van is the visionary of the Sylvia Woods Empire. Brenda and Van were inspired to write this book by their beloved mother, Mrs. Sylvia Woods.

Meet the Illustrator

Laurel Tyndale is an illustrator and graphic designer who has lived and worked in New York City for the past thirty years. He graduated from Pratt Institute.

Printed in the United States
By Bookmasters